MODERN SUFI POETRY

DEBORAH BELL

PARAS

1994

Published by
PARAS,
BM Box 6596,
London WC1N 3XX.

Cover and book design: Deborah Bell
Illustrations: © Deborah Bell
Book ornament: © Deborah Bell
Set in Times

Printed and bound in England by
The Ipswich Book Company,
Nacton Road, Ipswich,
Suffolk IP3 9QR

British Library Cataloguing in Publication Data
   Bell, Deborah
   Who Sees The Wind
   Modern Sufi Poetry
   1. Title
   821.914

ISBN 1 874292 03 5

Dedicated to
all the Great Ones
who have paved the
way and made the
impossible
possible.

The wind bloweth where
it listeth, and thou hearest
the sound thereof,
but canst not tell whence
it cometh, and whither it goeth:
so is every one that is born
of the spirit.

Jesus

CONTENTS

Contents

Contents

The heavens are still; no sound.
where then shall God be found?
search not in distant skies;
in man's own heart He lies.

Confucius

Prayer is a silent surrendered place
Where no words come to play,
It is a step into the endless sky –
To die.
Prayer is emptiness,
A meeting with the Guest,
A dance,
A gratitude,
A joy.

There is only that Infinite, Nameless,
and you cannot imprison it by
giving it any name at all.
Irina Tweedie

I laugh sometimes
At the things that I do
And my mind can't make any sense of it,
I laugh sometimes
At the things that I see
And my mind can't make any sense of it,
I laugh sometimes
At the way life unfolds
And my mind can't make any sense of it.

O that I may leave
This tavern for drunks,
Put down my glass
Stop the search for the pathless path,
The narrow way of no return,
Not to fly
Not to be,
Not to see,
Gone,
No other shore
No me no more.

I remembered the forgotten embrace,
The tearing asunder,
The sacrifice,
And I wept
And I wept
And I wept tears from the heart of my soul,
Never known such pain;
O my Beloved,
I had forgotten that perfect embrace,
That tearing asunder,
The sacrifice,
And I wept
And I wept
And I wept.

These tears that come to my eyes
Are a moment of gratitude to You,
This ecstasy that wells within me
Is a passionate moment with You,
This stillness that descends
Is the silence of merging with You.
O my Beloved these words can not say
How you rendered me naked
So empty inside
So filled with You.

Where no one could reach,
You have touched me;
You are the rains of descending grace,
You are the joy of my heart,
You are this silent moment,
Nothing can tear us apart.

For me it was always about the Truth,
It was just that I did not know it,
I always wanted more
Than what I saw in front of me
But I did not know where to find it;
When I saw my Teacher
I knew I was there with the Truth,
Then what I saw in front of me
Was enough.

The heart is where
All judgement and fear
Disappear.
The heart is an open space
The endless sky,
Where you die.

The roads to God are as many as
human beings, as many as the breaths
of the children of man.

Sufi saying

This longing
Is You reminding me of You,
This fullness
Is You reminding me of You,
This beauty
Is You reminding me of You,
This atrocity
Is You reminding me of You,
In whatever You do
Is You reminding me of You

So much nostalgia,
So much living in the past
Many saying it was better than today,
Does distance make it all seem better?
Was not yesterday once today!

What I know now
I learnt at a school
Where nothing is said
And all is known

Is there a valley called rage?
If not, then I name one so.
I stand in this valley of rage, pure rage,
Howling,
Baying at the sun that has faded away,
I have only rage at god today,
Rage, pure rage turning to the helplessness
Of knowing that only divine grace
Can set me free,
Raging,
Crying at God –
Help me.

Only one master –
This world,
Or the next!

To say that Sufis
Are the Lovers of God,
To say that Sufis
Are the Fools of God,
To say that Sufis
Are the Friends of God
Does not come close
To the reality
Of that which it really is.

Silence is looking for us with
the urgency of a lover.
Llewellyn Vaughan-Lee

I held in my hand a goblet
It was filled with the finest of wine,
It's colour was gold, pure wonder
Distilled from beyond any time,
The aroma was made in heaven
It tasted pure and divine;
My heart thanked God in silence
As the nectar passed my lips
I felt so warmed, so loved, so blessed –
Drunk was I beyond bliss.

Now is the time to remember
The promise made long long ago
To live life in its highest dimensions.
In love, in wonder, in grace,
O let me never never forget
That I am on a journey back home;
Home is where it's always the Oneness
The source of All Being, All Seeing;
Now is the time to remember
That life is a spiritual journey –
A journey home;
O let me never never forget,
That I am a child of the Light.

Interweave my heart with Yours
I asked the weaver of life,
Interweave my soul with Yours
With threads of golden light.
Interweave Your Truth in me
Your Joy, Your Bliss, Your Sight.
Interweave the day and night
Till I disappear into You
Into the All and Nothingness
The One, the True.

Who will reflect my love to me,
Was the cry of my human soul.
Who will live and die for me,
Was the cry of my human heart.
Who will cross the river with me,
Was the cry of my human mind:
What is the point of this self torture
I had came to the end of the line;
Then I felt a presence surround me,
And for the very first time
I knew that life was supporting me,
With love, and showers of grace,
I knew there was no going back
To pointing the finger outside,
All that I hoped and longed for
I knew I had to find inside.

There is a valley where there is nothing but
Confusion, despair, torment and pain.
It's the valley of bewilderment.
O that I could have stood there in prayer
And deep gratitude,
And accepted that this was The Now.
But while in there I was so entangled
And my life was in such disarray,
Later I came to understand
What all the mystics say –
That bewilderment is a stage on the way;
But while in there it seems like forever
Like there's no lightness no love and no grace,
All that I hoped and longed for was –
Please let me out of this space.

Be empty my heart, be empty.
Be empty of all that is I,
All attachments must go –
To pleasure
To gain
To pain,
Even to sensitivity,
To all that is of this world
Nothing must remain –
Be less than the dust on my feet,
Be less than a grain of sand,
Die while living,
That is the price that is asked,
For Nirvana it's a price worth giving.

Your smile is a worth a thousand smiles
Your look cut to help me feel,
Your heart melts a multitude
Your love my heart did steal,
You held me in your tender hands
And threw me to the winds,
You saw me shake and cry and pain
And fall and slip and slide,
You helped me crawl and walk again
Compassion always your guide.

To Irina Tweedie
Deepest gratitude

Melt melt my frozen heart,
Melt into the ocean of love,
Drop by drop I watch you thaw,
Drop by drop I surrender more.

The Friend who lives in my house
is the lover of my Heart.
Rabi'a

Travelling the road less travelled,
Brings one away from the crowd,
There is less and less to carry,
There is less and less to be found.

This life is a mystery,
To think it is something else
Is pure arrogance of the mind.

It is the longing,
The longing for That that carves the road
Which goes beyond the known,
It is the longing for That which cuts
Through the darkness of our being,
It takes us Home,
Home to the Great Beloved,
To where we all belong,
It is a passion song.

It was not just the looking
That left me bare,
Silent love affair;
A wonder struck,
A feeling welled so deep
So pregnant;
To move towards you
Was such a silent joy;
O life
How beautiful you manifest
In the blossom of a tree,
No word came near me,
How it is I can't explain,
I only know that to see you
My heart felt so much,
So much,
So much.

Windows frost with patterns
Calling snow queens from
Russian story books.

From a white grey sky
The snow falls
And the winds carry it to the ground,
No sound,
Just big white flakes
Falling
Falling
Falling.

Did you ever wonder why
And from where the moment came,
And called you to look –
There a moon so full shone
Clearing the verbal chatterings
Of the mind,
Capturing one's being so totally
That standing there was one with time,
Or maybe it was a moon so new
That it's line curved to awaken
The timelessness of one's hidden splendour,
Awe, and the depths of stars twinkling
Made motionless a child in wonder.

Always I find my being thankful
To have eyes to see a sun set
Or a moon rise,
O let me dissolve totally with the sun
To rise again new –
Not to carry yesterday in my today.

The One God is hidden in
all living beings.
Vedas

To respond to life's situations,
Not to react,
That is what life wants of me,
It's the way of non being,
This way is seeing that I am not in control,
That I do not determine the eternal flow,
My responsibility is that I am responsible
To respond or react to what life brings to me.

When the fire of desire rises higher
And the longing for love reaches truth,
When ones meaning for living unfolds further
And a peace starts to take root,
Then outside externals don't matter,
One knows that it all fades with time,
When the heart belongs to no other
Then for the Beloved one wants only to shine.

Something sublime has started to echo,
Some call it the Absolute,
Some call it Truth,
Something divine has started to blossom
God has taken root.

My lover is divine
He showed Himself to me,
It was in a moment of deep silence
That His heart talked to mine
The touch was sublime –
Pure ecstasy,
All that I knew of as love
Is no more
I have been shown another shore.

It was not an ache in my heart
It was a devastating pain.
I cried and died.
Purify this heart with fire divine
O the pain of love, today is mine.

So many tears have I cried for You,
So many songs have I sung for You,
How many deaths do I die for You?
O my heart aches and breaks for You,
How much longer can I wait for You?

The unknown sings to my heart
And beckons its song to reside there,
It's ecstasy longs to be all that I am
It's calling me, calling me.
I am a boat whose sails are filled
With the winds of longing,
My compass is my Teacher,
My destination –
God.

The Lord is my shepherd;
I shall not want.
Psalm 23

Blessings of understandings come
When there is a deep surrender to Him,
There comes a knowing of something
That moves me;
Learning to be nothing is a divine grace
Cannot be done by the will,
Only in a deep surrender
Is there the blessing of knowing
That I am not the doer
That I am not the weaver of time.

So deep is the loss of
Letting illusions go,
I am crossing over
Leaving this world behind,
The beyond calls,
I have to go.

A few simple words can turn a heart forever.
Simple statements from my teacher
Still reverberating
Becoming part of me,
The blessings of spiritual life.
Once she said –
You know what it's like to be in love,
To myself I said, I do,
Then She said –
THIS is a thousand times better!
Within an instant I answered,
I'll have that too.

O the joy of seeing
The blossoms on the trees
Multiply .

Great Teachers
Help us to know the ways of love,
Help us to know
The deeper longings of the heart,
Help us to part from lesser fruits
Help us to reap eternal truths.

A great drunkard beckoned,
For the wine we went,
We drank all night and day
Hours slipped away,
A finger was pointed to the moon
Hearts were warmed in the sun –
Nectar,
Lead turns to gold,
We hear stories our ancestors told,
We belong to the faithfuls fold;
We are Sufis
Nomads of centuries old,
For the ways of this world we do not care
We ask only our love to share.

Listen to the voice
That has no sound,
Follow the road
That can not be seen,
Long for reality
Not for the world,
Sing the song that
Can not be heard.
Go to the place
That is not found,
Dance in the air
Stand on the ground.

Every where one turns
Gravity pulls,
Every where one turns
Levitation pulls –
What a tension !

What encouragements
There are along the way;
What treasures, what gifts,
With an open heart
A deep longing for Oneness
A trust that there is Truth,
We can learn to understand
What the Great Ones say.

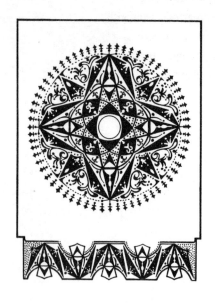

You who change all things
cannot be changed.
St. Augustine

With God's divine grace
We learn ease of movement
To a space of non doing,
It is something to long for,
It is something to learn
From the Masters of Truth;
First we hear the hint,
Then take up the challenge,
Then trust being guided;
All the Great Ones
Show us this way,
It is up to us to want it.

New understandings
Take us
To new understandings.

You can have all your bricks and your mortar
All your finery, your gold, your awards,
There is only one thing that matters to me
And that is the truth of what is;
How could I ever forsake the wisdom
That comes from the beginnings of time,
The beauty of Truth is sublime;
Never O never to waver,
To be mindful, never to doubt,
Listening, learning to savour the Truth –
This is what I care about.

Pride in God !
My heart feels it,
Yet it's beyond even that,
It's a fullness felt,
And yet no interpretations
Are really possible,
All I know is that
One can come to know
This pride in God.

In a moment of grace
My love found me,
He is the Lord of the full moon
The lord of the inner sky,
My love is the one who does not die.

At night falling into You –
Fathomless depths.
At night merging into You –
Endless skies.
At night dissolving into You
My heart sings with You
Love divine.

Through
We share
Through
We see.

When one has looked everywhere
And found no lasting peace.
When this world becomes a hollow lonely place,
When the heart shatters,
Cries and cries and dies to what is known –
Then the deeper recesses of the heart are shown,
In these chambers the alone meets the alone,
A sanctuary found
The falcon on the ground sees its feathers shorn –
A time to mourn;
A time to tend the wounds,
To wait,
To fall at the feet of the Great Ones.
To learn again to rise,
To echo the call.

The path unfolds like night turning day,
And the way becomes the slow grinding down
Of learning surrender to something greater than I.
The path and the way become every instant,
Every day of being fully here and attentive,
Feet on the ground.
And the way and the day become
The Thread of Remembrance –
Always focused Else Where:
It is not something fathomed, understood;
When it is found – it is lost.
And my Fathers are well pleased.

Just remember that I am,
and that I support the entire cosmos
with only a fragment of my being.
The Bhagavad Gita

This mystery of making space
For the Divine to descend
Brings light to the self
Brings love to the heart,
Let me be whole
Let me be One.

Watching the way the water flows
And glides between the rocks,
Watching the way it bends and turns,
One learns non attachment.

Watching the ways of the trees
Giving their fragrance and fruits,
Watching their way of not knowing,
One learns over flowing.

Watching the ways of the clouds
Moving in the sky,
Watching the way they change their shape,
One learns dissolve to die.

Watching the ways of The Great Ones
Those with no features and no face,
Watching the ways of these Buddhas,
One learns the ways of grace.

Deborah Bell/O'Brien was born in Dublin, Ireland in 1946. She was educated at the Irish National College of Art & Design. In 1986 she had a call to move to London. Six months later she found herself at the feet of Irina Tweedie of the Mujaddidiyya Line of the Naqshbandiyya Order of Sufism. They are known as the Golden Sufis, the Silent Sufis. Since then Deborah has been guided by this line and tradition. She knows that to be a Sufi is more than a way of life, it is to be embraced by the very Heart of the universe. The Sufi way is referred to as *the way of the heart*, they are also known as *the people of the path* and *the lovers and friends of God*. Deborah lives as a craftsperson in North London, occasionally giving readings from the Mystics and her own work. She has three children, two daughters and a son.

We go to the Absolute Truth in silence,
for it can be found only in silence, and it is Silence.
That is why we are called the Silent Sufis.
Irina Tweedie